What If JESUS Told The Truth?

Allen W. Fleming

DEDICATION

I dedicate this book to my best friend and King, Jesus.

I also dedicate this book to my wife Teresa and my adult children, Reasey and Matthew Lee and Ben and Meg Fleming, who stood by me through the trials and tribulations of creating an independent ministry.

This book came to being because of all of the partners and friends of Know Jesus Know Grace.com whose faithful and generous financial support and encouragement made it possible and to them also I dedicate this book.

Finally, to Brant Bateman, Mike Cottrell, Ed Everett, Wynn Everett, Jim Exley, Brant Frost, Eron Helfin, Henry Hine, Dr. Michael Howard, Larry King, Jeff Jordan, Jeff Lantz, Jim Lyons, Mel McBride, Ken Minchew, Dwayne Samples, Scott Smith, Terell Smith, Eric Swartz, and Gary Wallace for your faithful support I dedicate this book to you.

Pastor Allen Fleming

Table of Contents

ACKNOWLEDGMENTS

With gratitude to God for telling me to write this book.

With gratitude to Jesus and the Holy Spirit for instructing me in the Word.

With gratitude to the following Apostles, Prophets, Pastors, Evangelists, Teachers, Sponsors, Mentors and Friends who have contributed to this book: Dal Korn, Bill Gibson, Bill Wilson, Paul Crum, Buddy Crum, Mary Crum, Dwight Keith, Jerry Thomas, Ron Reeser, Loyd Skidmore, Preston Haag, Andrew Womack and Kenneth E. Hagin.

With gratitude to all of the partners past, present and future of Throne of Grace Ministries and Know Jesus Know Grace. Com who make my work possible.

With gratitude to Gregory Scott Lauman and Laimon Godel for guiding me through the process of finishing this work.

Pastor Allen Fleming

FOREWORD

This book is a compilation of messages given to me by the Holy Spirit. God encouraged and exhorted me to write the Words that He gave to me and I tried to eliminate as much of my flesh as possible.

The Gospel of Jesus is the most wonderful message the world has ever known. God came to the earth in the person of Jesus to deliver the glorious news that we are reconciled to Him through accepting Jesus as our Lord and Savior.

The Good News is that now we can inherit eternal salvation just by believing in Jesus. We also receive great and precious promises. The Gospel of Jesus should make us jump for joy when we read it! If you need uplifting and happiness in your life read the Gospel.

Do you know that by accepting Jesus as the King of our lives that we are found not guilty before God?

As you read the Gospel of Jesus you should be happier than a kid on Christmas Eve!

Jesus reveals to us through His Gospel that our relationship with Him is based on the sacrificial death of Jesus to pay the complete price for our sins. We are no longer under a works based relationship with Him. Jesus has through our belief in Him made us Holy, Blameless and Beyond Correction in His sight.

"For it is by grace that you have been saved through faith, and that is not of yourselves it is a gift from God, not of works lest any man should boast" (Ephesians 2:8&9)

"Therefore since we are justified (acquitted, declared righteous, and given a right standing with God) through faith, let us [grasp the fact that we have the peace of reconciliation to hold and to enjoy] peace with God through our Lord Jesus Christ"

"Through Him also we have access (entrance, introduction) by faith into this grace (God's willingness ability and power that has done for us what we can not or will not do for ourselves) in which we now stand, and let us rejoice and exult in our hope of experiencing (in this life and the life to come) the Glory of God."

(Romans 5:1&2)

As you read on, remember that Jesus is His Word. He has guaranteed its truth with His own blood.

"In the beginning [before all time] was the Word (Christ) and the Word was God Himself. He was present originally with God. All things were made and came into existence through Him; and without Him was not even one thing made that has come into being." (John 1:1-3)

The purpose of satan is to bring into question the Word of God. He knows that Jesus is the Word. He wants to render Jesus powerless in the lives of His children through unbelief and doubt in the Word.

Through the teachings in this book, I want to aggravate the hell out of those who refuse to believe Jesus. Their eternal lives depend on it.

You see, the only way to God is through Jesus. No other religion offers a path to righteousness with God that does not require the impossible task of standing before God on the basis of one's performance.

Jesus is the only way!

"Jesus said to him, I am the Way and the Truth and the Life; no one comes to the Father except through Me." (John 14:6)

Jesus meant and guaranteed every Word that came from His mouth. He left us a vast and powerful inheritance, which we receive by faith.

My goal is to see you walking in joy, peace, happiness and health beyond mortal comprehension. I want to see you going around in a state of joy and grace by reading in this book the truth of the wonderful life that Jesus promised us!!!

"Let us then fearlessly and confidently and boldly draw near to the throne of grace, that we may receive mercy and find grace to help in good time for every need [appropriate and well-timed help, coming just when we need it.] (Hebrews 4:16)

As you read on, imagine how wonderful life would be if you and the rest of the people of the world were to come to believe that Jesus Told The Truth!

Chapter 1 - What if Jesus told the truth

This may seem like a ridiculous title for a book, but what I have found is that even most Christians do not believe that Jesus told the truth.

Whenever I teach the gospel, I ask of the assembled, how many believe in Jesus. Invariably, everyone raises their hands. The follow up question is... "how many believe Jesus?" Again, all hands are raised. Then, I report the teachings of Jesus. At the close of the teaching period, I repeat the second question. The response this time is always different. The second time I ask the question, less hands are raised.

When people hear some of the things that Jesus actually taught their reaction ranges from acceptance and belief to unbelief and anger at the teacher for having dared utter the teachings. The more aggressive of the negative responders, are usually those who have been taught in traditional Christian churches.

The purpose of this writing is to lead the reader to consider what their life, their family's life and what this world would be like if Jesus really did mean literally the things that He said, and if indeed they were all true.

You may have been in church all of your life and right now be bristling at the idea of anyone questioning your belief level or the quality of your education. You may be Islamic or Buddhist, or Jewish or atheist or agnostic. I am not asking you to make a decision to believe Jesus right now. I am asking you to consider the cost to you of making a decision to believe Him. What if indeed He told the truth? What would the truth then be, and what would it mean to you?

I do not claim to be the world's foremost authority on the teachings of Jesus. However, I have been teaching His gospel for many years. As a result, the gospel of Jesus has become truth to me. It is a fantastic and to me, very real hope of joy and peace and strength in this life, and in the life to come. My prayer is that as you continue reading you will find whatever you seek from God in the Word of His Son.

Please understand, You do not have to be a Christian now or at any point, as you read this book, to consider the question that you are being asked. What if Jesus was telling the truth?

In order to answer the question, it would be well to know what the gospel of Jesus is. From here on, I will do my best to communicate in simple form the essence of His teaching. There are some assumptions that will be necessary to accept. Use your imagination with these as you did as a child. If the assumptions are not acceptable to you at this present moment, pretend that they are until you have enough information to either accept or reject them. Please do not reject the basic assumptions until you have heard their basis.

Here are the basic assumptions necessary to follow this report of the teachings of Jesus:

(1)   That God is.

(2)   That all people do, and think things that are unacceptable to God. We will further refer to these things as sins.

(3)   That because God is Holy and can not accept sin in any form, no person can stand before God based on their performance.

(4)   That because all people have fallen short of God's required holiness by virtue of their sin, that without a savior, a mediator who is holy and therefore able to intercede for them, they are without the capacity to enter God's presence.

(5)   That the payment for sin is eternal separation from God and condemnation to the place known as hell. Hell being the place of eternal absence from hope or mercy or grace, it is a place of perpetual torment without relief. It is the realm of the evil one. Those who enter, are there for eternity.

(6)   That there is, and has been one who comes but for to kill, to steal, and to destroy. This one is constantly at work using the only power he has, which is to deceive. The goal of the evil one is to deceive people into not believing the Word of God. He will be referred to further as satan.

(7)   That God loved the world and its people so much that He sent His son into the world to save it from its sins. That whosoever would believe on Him would never perish, but would have by virtue of their belief, everlasting life.

(8)   That Jesus came into the world taught the world the plan of salvation and blessing, was beaten and tortured, put to death by being hung on a cross, died, and rose from the dead. After which, he rose from the dead and in the presence of hundreds of witnesses; walked, talked, taught and did many miracles. Then after forty days, He ascended to the Father.

(9)   That if you believe in your heart that God raised Jesus from the dead, and you confess with your mouth that God raised Jesus from the dead, you will be saved. For with the heart, we believe unto righteousness and with the mouth we confess and are saved.

(10)   That in His death burial and resurrection, Jesus paid the price for the sins of all people, once for all.

If you cannot accept these truths at the present moment, read on and pretend that you have. They are the cornerstones of this book. The job of the author is not to convince you that the Word of God is correct, but to present the Word to the reader. The reader is given the opportunity to accept or reject the Word, because God's will for us is that we use our gift of free will to choose.

Chapter 2 – The Great Deception

I recently had a conversation with another author about the title of this book. The author smirked and replied that the title is senseless.

He stated that every Christian believes Jesus and consequently believes that He told the truth. "Really I asked?" "Do you believe Jesus?" I asked.

"Yes of course I do!" He replied. I asked my friend if he was sure that he believed everything that Jesus said. He replied that he did not know everything that Jesus said.

"Well, that is certainly the truth" I replied. The sources of ignorance of the Word are many. They include but are not limited to poor teaching, negligent teaching, lack of teaching, lack of interest and unbelief.

John wrote of Jesus that if all that Jesus said and did had been reported there would not be enough books in all the libraries in the world to contain them.

I asked my friend if he actually knew all that Jesus said, if he would believe him. "Of course I would!" he insisted. However, as I began to teach the man what Jesus declared as fact, he balked. It turns out he not only does not believe the teachings of Jesus, He resents them.

Do you think that most Christians are more advanced in their belief of the teachings of Jesus? Personally, I don't think most Christians know very much about what Jesus taught, because they have not been taught them or they have been taught them incorrectly. I am not blaming student or teacher. We are all products of what we have been taught.

Let us consider one of the most elementary teachings of Jesus. From the 1st Gospel of John the disciple. John 14:12... "Verily, Verily...(truthfully, truthfully) I, (as in the great I AM, I the Son of God, I the creator of all things in heaven and in earth, I the one who was and is and is to come, I the first born among the brethren, I the brightness of the glory of God and the exact image of his person, that I) say to you,(us) He that believeth on me, the works that I do shall he do also; (Pause and consider what our Lord and Savior the same who taught us our John 3:16 scripture is saying. We say that we believe Jesus, He is saying that if we do, we shall do the same works that He did. That would include raising the dead, healing all nature of diseases among the people, commanding all of God's creation to obey him, casting out demons and more things than can be contained in all the books and libraries in the world.)

"and greater works than these shall he do; (Woah, Hoss...What would be greater works than those we just considered? That would be leading others to salvation and baptizing them in the Holy Ghost.) "because I go to my Father". (Because Jesus paid the full price to reconcile us to God, We are now made righteous by faith in him and have become a royal priesthood and joint heirs with Jesus and we not only are empowered to do the same works that he did, but even greater works.) How are we doing on the believing Jesus part?

This scripture is one of the reasons that to pray for God to expand our borders or give us favor, or to bless us, is error. He has empowered us to do and be greater in this earth than He was. Let us continue with this teaching. "And whatsoever (the nature of the word whatsoever eliminates any man developed qualifications such as "yes but it must be in God's will" a thought totally inconsistent with the Gospel of Jesus. Whatsoever is the ultimate total inclusion? The word whatsoever is the opposite of yes but.) you shall ask in my name, that will I do , (please note here that there are no performance based qualifiers such as...if you did not do or say something bad, or ...unless you are in sin, or if you are a disciple, or if you are in right standing with God, or if...your motives are pure, or if it is good for you, or if it be his will.) that the Father may be glorified through the Son"." If you ask anything (please note the lack of qualifiers like...If you pass the test, or after you go through the process, or if it is in God's time, or unless it is for something you desire, money etc.) I will do it."

Jesus also taught us saying...." Have faith in God, For verily I say unto you, That whosoever shall say unto this mountain, Be thou removed, and be thou cast into the sea; and shall not doubt in his heart, but shall believe that those things which he saith shall come to pass; he shall have WHATSOEVER, he saith." Therefore, I say unto you what things soever ye desire, when ye pray, believe that ye receive them, and ye shall have them."

7

Jesus also taught us saying..." And these signs shall follow them that believe, In my name they shall cast out devils, they shall speak with new tongues; They shall take up serpents; and if they drink any deadly thing, it shall not hurt them; they shall lay hands on the sick, and they shall recover."

Jesus taught me these scriptures. Jesus taught much that is contrary to what we have always heard; which led me to the great question of this thesis. If Jesus was not insane or a liar, and he truly thought out and meant what he said, why have we never been taught this and why are we not walking in the power that he gave us? Why has the body of Jesus not accepted his teachings? Why are we dis-empowered? The answer is the subject of this teaching..."The Great Deception". At this point it is urgent for me to state as clearly as possible and pray that *you* will understand that this teaching is not a slap at the Church or any Pastor, denomination or fellowship. Please understand that we are all products of what we have been taught and the traditions that have been passed to us. I am merely being led of The Spirit to share with His Flock what he has revealed to me through the Word, So that we can begin to walk in the power that Jesus freely paid the high price to give us.

It is important to understand that at the time Jesus came to earth there were two groups of people in the earth, the Jews and the Gentiles. Everyone on earth falls into one of these categories.

The Jews had rejected God and placed themselves under the Law. The Gentiles were never under the law and have never been. They were lost and without God or hope in this world. Thank God that," For God so loved the world that he gave his only begotten son, that whosoever believeth in him shall not perish, but shall have everlasting life". (John 3:16)

How did the law (the Ten Commandments and its 600 associated ordinances and a performance based relationship with God, come to be? and to whom does it apply?) The answers are clearly stated in the scriptures.

Galatians 3:19" Wherefore then serveth the law? It was added because of transgressions, till the seed should come to whom the promise was made; and it was ordained by angels in the hand of a mediator. (It came because of transgressions which we will now list, till the seed Jesus should come to whom the promise was made, the Hebrews. It was ordained by angels in the hand of a mediator, Moses.) Clearly, the law came to the Hebrews and it was intended to be in effect for a specific time period, until the seed should come. And, it was created and given to those to whom the promise was given, the Hebrews.

What transgressions brought the law?

Exodus 14:11and12..." And they said unto Moses, because there were no graves in Egypt, hast thou taken us away to die in the wilderness? Wherefore hast thou dealt thus with us, to carry us forth out of Egypt? Is not this the word that we did tell thee in Egypt, saying, Let us alone, that we may serve the Egyptians? For it had been better for us to serve the Egyptians, than that we should die in the wilderness."

Exodus 16:2 and3..."And the whole congregation of the children of Israel murmured against Moses and Aaron in the wilderness: And the children of Israel said unto them, Would to God we had died by the hand of the Lord in the land of Egypt, when we sat by the flesh pots and when we did eat bread to the full; for ye have brought us forth into this wilderness, to kill this whole assembly with hunger."

Exodus 17:3 "And the people thirsted there for water; and the people murmured against Moses, and said, Wherefore is this that thou hast brought us out of Egypt, to kill us and our children and our cattle with thirst?"

The murmuring infuriated God and his wrath waxed hot against what God described as the "stiff necked Jews" as he heard them murmuring against him in their tents. But the ultimate act of unbelief and rebellion was this...

Exodus 20:19" And they said unto Moses, Speak thou with us and we will hear; but let not God speak with us, lest we die."

Deuteronomy 5:24 and 25...." And ye said, behold, the Lord our God hath shown us his glory and his greatness, and we have heard his voice out of the midst of the fire; we have seen this day that God doth talk with man, and that He liveth. Now therefore why should we die? For this great fire will consume us; if we hear the voice of the Lord our God any more then we shall die. For who is there of all flesh that heard the voice of the living God speaking out of the midst of the fire, as we have, and lived?

Deuteronomy 9:7 and 8..." Remember and forget not, how thou provoked the Lord thy God to wrath in the wilderness; from the day that thou didst depart out of the land of Egypt, until ye came unto this place, ye have been rebellious against the lord. Also in Horeb ye provoked the Lord to wrath, so that the Lord was angry with you to have destroyed you."

So, God's chosen people rejected his messenger first, the God himself in favor of his messenger. Since the people had rejected God they had to have some system to protect themselves from each other. Thus the Law. God was so angry with the Jews at this time that he told Moses that he wanted to kill them.

Moses reminded God that he could not kill them because he had made a covenant with Abraham that his seed would be mighty in the earth. God told Moses that he would kill the Jews and make Moses a nation unto himself. Moses interceded for his people telling God that if he killed the children of Israel, that the pagans would say that God had not kept his promise to his people and that he had betrayed them by killing them in the desert. God had to

11

protect the lineage of Jesus, the promised one, and he did so by sparing the Jews but by giving them the Mosaic Law and its ordinances which he knew were impossible to keep.

So, now that the people had chosen the Law over God, he gave them the Law. He instructed them to build an ark in which to keep the stone tablets on which the Law had been written by the hand of God. He then instructed them to hang a veil...Exodus 26:33..." And thou shalt hang up the veil under the taches, that thou mayest bring in thither within the veil, the ark of the testimony; and the VEIL SHALL DIVIDE UNTO YOU BETWEEN THE HOLY PLACE AND THE MOST HOLY." (The law would be placed in the ark and the veil around it would separate God's people from God, by their choice.)

Remember this scripture about the veil. It will be dealt with by Jesus.

What then of the Gentiles (us)? We were lost and without hope in the world.

Switching from the King James Version to the Amplified a more pure translation from the original Greek and Hebrew...Ephesians chapter 2 beginning in the 12th verse... "Remember that at that time you were., separated (living apart) from Christ (excluded from all part in Him); utterly estranged and outlawed from the rights of Israel as a nation, and strangers with no share in the sacred compacts of the (Messianic) promise with no knowledge of or right in God's agreements, His covenants. And you had no hope (no promise); you were in the world without God."

Jesus emphasized the fact that we are not and were never under the law in his teaching to the woman at Jacobs well. John 4:19" The woman (a gentile) saith unto him, Sir, I perceive that thou art a prophet. Our Fathers worshipped in this mountain; and ye say that in Jerusalem is the place where men ought to worship. (The Woman is reporting that Gentiles were prohibited from worshiping God. Jesus is about to confirm that she is correct according to the Law that He is about to change forever for the Gentiles).

Jesus said to her, " Woman, believe me, the hour cometh and now is when ye (us the Gentiles) shall neither in this mountain, nor yet at Jerusalem, worship the Father. Ye worship ye (us the Gentiles) know not what; we know what we worship; for salvation is of the Jews".

(Jesus is stating clearly and emphatically that the Gentiles were not included under the Law, He states without qualification that there was no plan or hope of salvation for the Gentiles at that time, but that because he would reconcile all men to God, they would soon be able to know and worship the same God.)

"But the hour cometh, and now is, when the true worshippers will worship the Father in spirit and in truth; for the Father seeketh such to worship Him. God is a Spirit; and they that worship him must worship him in spirit and in truth".

Another powerful and clear teaching from Jesus our Lord proclaiming that the Gentiles (us) were never under the law and its ordinances and were in fact without hope in the world.

From the Amplified Bible...Matthew 15:22-28...And behold, a woman who was a Canaanite (a Gentile) from that district came out and, with a (loud troublesomely urgent) cry, begged, Have mercy on me, O Lord, Son of David! My daughter is miserably and distressingly and cruelly possessed by a demon! But He did not answer her a word. And his disciples came and implored Him, saying; Send her away, for she is crying out after us. He answered; I was sent ONLY TO THE LOST SHEEP OF ISRAEL. (Jesus is clearly and emphatically stating that he was not sent to the Gentiles that they were lost.) But she came and, kneeling, worshipped Him and kept praying, Lord, help me! And he answered, It is not right to take the children's bread and throw it to the little dogs. She said, yes, Lord, yet even the little pups eat the crumbs that fall from their masters' table. Then Jesus answered her, O woman, great is your faith! Be it done for you as you wish. And her daughter was cured from that moment."

Jesus declared that even though the gentiles were lost, faith in Him, would be their salvation.

I pray that you now understand that at this time the Jews had placed themselves under the Law and that the Gentiles were not and never have been under a performance based relationship with God.

This is when John 3:16 came in... FOR GOD SO LOVED THE WORLD (All men both Jews and Gentiles) THAT HE GAVE HIS ONLY BEGOTTEN SON, THAT WHOSOEVER BELIEVETH IN HIM WOULD NEVER PERISH BUT WOULD HAVE EVERLASTING LIFE.

Now God set all men free from the works of the law and the bondage of self!

John 1:15...John (John the Baptist) bare witness of him, and cried saying, This was he of whom I spake (prophesied) He that cometh after me is preferred before me; for he was before me. And of his fullness have we all received GRACE FOR GRACE. For the law came from Moses, but GRACE AND TRUTH came by Jesus Christ.

So Jesus fulfilled the Law so that the Jews who were under it would be made free. "As many as received him, to them gave the power to become sons of God". (John 1:12)

Then Jesus reconciled all men Jews and Gentiles to himself by his punishment, death on the cross, burial, dissension and resurrection." If I be lifted up from the earth, will draw ALL men unto me". (John 12:32)

Here is where the separated Gentiles were joined to Jesus and reconciled to God. "Surely he bore our griefs and carried our sorrows (picture Jesus being judged, punished beaten and then carrying the cross) Yet, we considered him stricken, smitten of God and afflicted. But he was wounded for our transgressions, he was bruised for our iniquities; the chastisement of our peace was upon him; and with his stripes we are healed." Isaiah 53:4and5

Remember the veil representing the law that God commanded to be hung to separate the Hebrews who had placed themselves under the law from God, in Exodus 26:33?

"Jesus when he had cried again with a loud voice, yielded up the ghost. AND BEHOLD THE VEIL OF THE TEMPLE WAS RENT IN TWAIN (Torn in half) FROM THE TOP TO THE BOTTOM." (Matthew 27:50 and 51) At the instant Jesus died, The veil representing the law that separated the Jews from God was torn in half and nothing was between them and God.

The Law had been fulfilled.

So, at the moment Jesus died, the Jews were made free from the law, all of its ordinances and a performance based relationship with God; because he was the only human who ever fulfilled the Law. Now the Jews could be completely justified to God by Faith in Jesus. The Gentiles who were never responsible for the Law and its ordinances and whom had no relationship with God, were also justified unto righteousness by faith in Jesus. Now no humans were separated from God by their performance of law or ordinances or their degree of obedience. Now the mediator between God and Man is Jesus and his righteousness.

At the moment of Jesus' death, the old covenant was fulfilled. The new covenant began in Acts chapter 2 verse 4 when the promise of the Holy Spirit fell on the Apostles. Now God's new relationship with all mankind is Grace through faith not performance.

This is where the great deception began. The devil could not stand by and see all mankind made free from the bondage of self. So he deceived Jesus' own disciples. They had been given power and authority by the Holy Spirit as Jesus had promised to become his witnesses to Judea and to the ends of the earth. Satan had to work fast so he convinced the disciples to add the works of the law and ordinances and a works or obedience or performance quotient to the plan of salvation. He thoroughly deceived the disciples and off they went teaching faith mixed with performance.

The deception of the original disciples and how they went among the early church falsely teaching performance or law mixed with faith is clearly reported by Luke in the 15th chapter of the book of

Acts and by Paul in the 2nd chapter of the letter to the Church at Galatia. Here is a direct quotation from Galatians 2:14 " But when I saw that they walked not uprightly according to the truth of the Gospel, I said unto Peter (representing the original disciples), before them all, If thou being a Jew, liveth after the manner of the Gentiles, and not as do the Jews, why compellest thou the Gentiles to live as do the Jews?" Paul asked the greatest question ever asked outside of Jesus." Peter if you are a Jew and you can't keep the Law and live under a performance based relationship with God, how can you put it on the Gentiles who were never under the law to begin with?"

God needed an Apostle who would preach the truth. He appointed the most vile of all sinners Saul of Tarsus who became Paul...The Teacher To The Gentiles (Us) we the Gentiles have two appointed Teachers...Jesus and Paul. What was so important that God and Jesus and the Holy Spirit had to reveal to us through Paul that they had to use him instead of the disciples?

"Nevertheless, brethren, I have written the more boldly unto you in some sort, as putting you in mind, because of the grace that is given to me of God, That I should be THE MINISTER OF JESUS CHRIST TO THE GENTILES; ministering the Gospel of God, that the offering up of the Gentiles (us) might be acceptable, being justified by the Holy Ghost." (Romans 15:15and16)

Here are a few of the urgent teachings from the Apostle Paul as revealed to him by the Holy Spirit and sent to us.

"It is by Grace **(God's willingness, ability and power to do those things for us that we, can not or will not do for ourselves)**. That you have been saved through Faith **(Living in**

this present moment with joyful expectation of the things that you can not see) that you have been saved. And that (Faith) is not of yourselves it is a gift from God not of works, lest any man should boast." (Ephesians 2:8and9)

"Therefore being justified (being found not guilty) by faith, we have peace with God, through our Lord Jesus Christ; by whom we have access into this grace wherein we stand and rejoice in hope of the glory of God." (Romans 5:1)

"Knowing that a man is not justified by the works of the law, but by faith in Jesus Christ, even we have believed in Jesus Christ, that we might be justified by THE FAITH OF JESUS CHRIST, and not by the works of the law; for by the works of the law, shall no flesh be justified. For I through the law am dead to the law, that I might live in God.

I am crucified with Jesus; NEVERTHELESS I LIVE; YET NOT I, BUT CHRIST LIVETH IN ME; AND THE LIFE I NOW LIVE IN THE FLESH, I LIVE BY THE FAITH OF THE SON OF GOD, WHO LOVED ME AND GAVE HIS LIFE FOR ME. I DO NOT FRUSTRATE THE GRACE OF GOD; FOR IF RIGHTEOUSNESS COME BY THE LAW, THEN JESUS IS DEAD IN VAIN". (Galatians 2:15 and 16 and 19-21)

Many of us believe that we understand this teaching and that we are not operating under the law. Here it is urgent to understand that Paul is talking about any type of performance based standard of trying to please God by our behavior. Many of us have even been taught that while we were saved unto salvation by Grace, that to be blessed we must be "good". Good can mean anything from trying to keep the 10 commandments that we were never under to begin with, or not having lustful or evil thoughts, or any stretch of the imagination of that spectrum.

Paul our teacher speaks directly to the notion that while we were saved by grace our life in the flesh is to be one of "obedience" or works or performance, in Colossians chapter 2:6 "As you received Christ Jesus your Lord, so walk ye in him." (We received Him by grace through faith).

Paul was our teacher sent from God with the message that the New Covenant with God is based on the complete work of Jesus and not on our performance. From Romans through

Hebrews, Paul intellectually and spiritually proclaims that the new covenant, established by Jesus through his blood, (Luke 22:20) is Grace through Faith. That our relationship with God is no longer about us but entirely about him.

However, Paul gives us dire warning in his letter to the Church of Galatia of the consequences of placing ourselves in a works or obedience or performance based relationship with God.

Here are the two dire warnings from Paul to us." So those who be of faith are blessed with faithful Abraham. For as many as are of the works of the law ARE UNDER A CURSE, for it is written. Cursed (the curses of being under and failing to keep 100% of the law may be found in Deuteronomy 8:15) is every one that continueth not in ALL things that are written in the book of the law to do them. But no man is justified by the law in the sight of God it is evident for, THE JUST SHALL LIVE BY FAITH. AND THE LAW IS NOT OF FAITH; BUT, THE MAN THAT DOETH THEM SHALL LIVE IN THEM." (In simpler speech, if you live by the law, you perish by the law.) Galatians 3:9-11

Finally, Paul answers through the revelation of the Holy Spirit why we are not walking in Jesus' prophecy of John 14:12..."Behold, I Paul (asserting his position as the appointed of God the Father, Jesus our Lord and The Holy Spirit teacher to us the Gentiles) say unto you that if you be circumcised (submit yourself again to a works based relationship with God) Jesus shall profit you nothing. For I testify again to every man that is circumcised, that he is a debtor to the whole law. CHRIST IS BECOME OF NO EFFECT TO YOU, WHOSOEVER OF YOU ARE JUSTIFIED BY THE LAW, YE ARE FALLEN FROM GRACE." (Galatians 5:2-4)

There is the answer to the original question...Why are we the body of Jesus disempowered? Because we have been deceived throughout time by the evil one. Paul calls it being "bewitched" in the 3rd chapter of Galatians into believing that we must improve on the work of Jesus by our behavior. Thereby, accomplishing his goal of devaluing the blood of Jesus.

We have all been taught at one time or another by well-meaning but unlearned teachers that we must do something to please God. Here are a few examples: "go through the test" "complete the process" "be in God's will"" be this or be that" etc." Yes there is grace...BUT"

Of this concept, Paul writes that a little leaven, leaveneth the whole bunch.

How do we begin to walk in Grace through faith and reject the works based relationship that the evil one has conned us into? We make a decision to Believe that Jesus[1] righteousness and faith in him accesses the Grace in which we now stand. Where do we get faith? The faith of the Son of God was given to you in full measure at the very second that you accepted Jesus as your Lord and Savior. How do we use the faith that we have been given? We make a decision to live one moment at a time with joyful expectation of the things that we cannot see.

Is there any such thing as a blocked blessing? Yes...unbelief and works will make Jesus of no effect in your life.

Is it really that simple and easy? It has to be so that all people can understand and operate in it.

What about sin mister Grace teacher? Are you saying that God blesses a mess? I am not saying that, Jesus did. He hath already given us all things that pertain to life and Godliness, he will not take what he has already given because his gifts and callings are without repentance. However, sin is a direct reflection of a lack of using faith and the level of unbelief in our lives. The more we believe the less we sin. The more we choose to walk in the free gift of faith that we have been given, the more we are changed into the likeness of Jesus. Unbelief does stop us from receiving.

What are the keys to the new covenant? Belief...making a decision to accept as true. Faith living one moment at a time with joyful expectation of the things we cannot see. (Hebrews 11:1) and Grace (accessed by choosing to live in faith) God's willingness ability and power to do those things for us that we can not or will not do for ourselves."

This teaching is life changing doctrine from Jesus and our appointed teacher Paul. Maybe you are having a challenge accepting it because it is not what you have been taught. Do not be upset with your teachers or with the author. Do not blame those who have taught you what they have been taught. Do not judge or condemn your teachers or parents because they did not know these things. Instead, if you have questions, use the Bible as the ultimate authority and remember the teaching of our Lord and Savior. "If you continue in my word, then indeed you are my disciple, and you shall know the truth, and the truth shall MAKE YOU FREE".

I pray that this teaching blesses you and that you will study and receive it. If you have been blessed by it, then pass it on to another who will be blessed.

With love to you all, your brother in Jesus, Pastor Allen

Chapter 3 THE SOURCE OF FAITH

We have been teaching a written series on what faith is and what it is not. We continued with how to employ faith. We broke faith down into its three components, (Hebrews 11:1 1. Now, living in this present moment, 2.With Hope/ Joyful expectation of 3.The Unseen).

We know that it is urgent to understand what faith is because we are required to live by faith. (Romans1:17& Galatians 3:11).

Since we have been justified (found not guilty), FREELY (not by our performance) by his GRACE (God's willingness ability and power to do those things for us that we can not or will not do for ourselves) through the redemption that is in Jesus Christ (Romans 3:24); We are the ones who are being required to live by faith.

Therefore, it would be well for us to know where to get faith. What then is the source of faith? Understandably, there is much confusion about this subject even within the body of Jesus. The reasons for the confusion are clear. We know who the author of confusion is and it is not Jesus. The evil one is still confusing the elect the same way he has since the beginning.

Satan tempted eve by bringing into question the Word of God. The statement he used then, he is still using today; "surely God did not say?"

The evil one has been twisting scriptures since the beginning of time. He has confused many of us from the pulpit. He has confused many of us with ignorance. He has confused many of us by deceiving us into accepting clichés instead of thoroughly studying the word.

Satan has been clouding the issue of faith forever. He does not want us to understand faith. Satan knows that the power to overcome him and receive the power and blessings that God has given the believers of Jesus is FAITH!

I was deceived by the lies and confused teachers and teachings caused by the evil one. There was a sense that faith could not come from human effort down inside of me and God revealed the truth to me through the Holy Spirit. I want to share the true source of faith with you

The evil one is powerless. He has been defeated in every way by Jesus. Jesus has given us dominion over all of the powers of the evil one. All satan can do is use our confusion and ignorance to deceive us. He has two goals. His goals are to devalue the blood of Jesus and to take away our testimony because with these two forces he is defeated.

The evil one devalues the blood of Jesus by making us believe that; Jesus' work on the cross was incomplete and that we must do things to improve on it. If we believe that we can add anything to the work of Jesus then His blood has no power in our lives because we are believing in our power instead of His.

Many of us have been taught that even our faith is under a performance standard. We have been taught that our faith can be expanded, grown or perfected. This teaching is based on the comments of Jesus regarding, "Great faith, ever increasing faith, little faith and no faith". If there are varying degrees of faith as described by our Lord then, it is assumed, that we must somehow progress through each of these levels.

However this entire proposition is based on an incorrect understanding of the ministry of Jesus. At the time Jesus was observing and commenting on these levels of faith, all men were operating in the flesh faith. So indeed they did have varying levels of Faith.

Our source of faith is Jesus. In the 12th chapter of Hebrews Paul our teacher appointed by God, explains that " Wherefore seeing that we are surrounded by such a great cloud of witnesses, let us lay aside every weight, and the sin that so easily besets us, and let us run the race with patience, looking unto JESUS who is the AUTHOR and FINISHER of our faith."

There is no ambiguity here. Jesus is clearly the Author and the Finisher of our faith. He began it and he ended it. How did he do this? By giving us His faith as a free gift that comes through belief in Him!

Ephesians 2:8 and 9..."For by Grace are you saved through Faith, and THAT IS NOT OF YOURSELVES, IT IS A GIFT FROM GOD NOT OF WORKS, LEST ANY MAN SHOULD BOAST. Paul our teacher appointed by God has made an unequivocal pronouncement guided by the Holy Spirit. Faith is a gift from God and it is not of works lest any man should boast. It was given as a free gift when you accepted Jesus as your Lord and Savior.

Once we accept Jesus we are given His faith as a free gift based on His righteousness and not through our efforts. Notice this statement from Peter to those who have chosen to believe Jesus:

"Simon Peter a servant and apostle (special messenger) of Jesus Christ, to those who HAVE RECEIVED (past tense) LIKE PRECIOUS FAITH with ourselves through the righteousness of God and our Savior Jesus Christ! " (2Peter 1:1)

Paul sums it up this way:

"May Blessing (laudation, praise and eulogy) be to the God and Father of our Lord Jesus Christ Who HAS (past tense) BLESSED US IN CHRIST WITH EVERY SPIRITUAL (given by the Holy Spirit) BLESSING IN THE HEAVENLY REALM!"

(Ephesians 1:3) Faith is a spiritual gift.

You see faith is a spiritual gift that is given to us in full measure by God through Jesus. It comes to us or we receive it when we accept Jesus. Follow this explanation from Paul:

"Because if you acknowledge and confess with your lips that Jesus is Lord and in your heart you believe (adhere to, trust in and rely on the truth) that God raise Him from the dead, you shall be saved."

"For with the heart a person believes and so is justified, and with the mouth he confesses and confirms his salvation.

"The scripture says, No man who believes in Him will ever be put to shame or be disappointed".

"No one for; there is no distinction between Jew and Gentile. The same Lord is Lord over all of us and He generously bestows His riches upon all who call upon Him in faith."

"For everyone who calls upon the name of the Lord will be saved."

"How then shall they call on him in whom they have not believed? And how shall they believe in him of whom they have not heard? And how shall they hear without a preacher? And how shall they preach unless they are sent? As it is written, how beautiful are the feet of those that preach the gospel of peace and bring glad tidings of good things?"

But they have not all obeyed the gospel (believed Jesus) for Isaiah said, Lord who hath believed our report?"

"So then faith comes by hearing [what is told], and what is heard comes by the preaching [of the message that came from the lips} of Christ (The Messiah Himself). "

(Romans 10:9-19)

These scriptures clearly state that salvation comes from hearing the gospel, the good news of what Jesus spoke and as a result of hearing, faith comes.

Unfortunately, many taking some words completely out of context, have drawn the incorrect conclusion that faith comes by "hearing and hearing". Their mistaken belief is that we must hear in the continual sense in order to get "more faith".

This incorrect assumption leads some to believe that if they haven't heard enough, they haven't enough faith to believe for a blessing or miracle. It is taught by some that the reason folks have not received a healing or a blessing; they must not have had enough faith. The inference being that they have not heard enough or grown enough or worked enough to have a high enough level of faith.

Nothing could be farther from the truth!!! Faith is a free gift from God and no gift from God is incomplete.

Some have been taught or believe that faith can be expanded or grown by, reading or hearing more scripture. This is not what the teaching says or is about. Go back to the 9th verse and ask the Holy Spirit to guide you in context through the 17th verse and you will see that this notion is mistaken.

This whole teaching is a direct statement that faith comes from accepting Jesus and being saved. It is clear that Paul is teaching that it is necessary to send teachers to teach the plan of salvation because from salvation comes faith.

Here is more clarity on the subject of the source of faith:

Romans 12:3 "For I say unto you, through the grace given unto me, to every man among you, not to think of himself more highly than he ought to think; but to think soberly, according as GOD HATH DEALT TO EVERY MAN THE MEASURE OF FAITH.

Romans 11:29 "For the gifts and callings of God are without repentance."

It is clear that Paul the teacher to the gentiles is telling us that Jesus is the source of our faith. That it is a free gift from him. Since it is a gift from God it cannot be taken away. Since Jesus began and ended it, it cannot be improved, enlarged or expanded.

Does faith come from hearing? Absolutely. You hear the gospel of Jesus. You confess with your mouth the Lord Jesus. You believe in your heart that God raised Jesus from the dead. You are given "The Measure" of faith as a free gift from God, not of works lest any man should boast. You receive all the faith you will ever need.

Our problem is not and has never been our lack of faith. All we need is faith as a grain of mustard seed and we can move mountains. Our problem is that we need to make a decision to walk in faith by choosing to live one moment at a time with joyful expectation of the things that we cannot see. Our challenge from Jesus is contained in Mark 11:22, 23 and 24.

How to receive from God by our Lord Jesus:

Mark 11:22...Step one..."Have faith in God."

Mark 11:23 Step two the challenge from the Great I AM in the person of Jesus. "I tell you the truth, that whosoever shall say to this mountain, be thou removed and be thou cast into the sea; and does not doubt in his heart, but believes that those things that he says shall come to pass; he shall have whatsoever he says."

There are no qualifications in this statement of truth from Jesus. Nowhere are there conditions of how good you are or varying degrees of faith or who your daddy is. Jesus is making a clear profound direction and stating a problem. The problem is the doubt in our hearts. He knows the problem. He is describing the problem and now he is about to state clearly without qualification the solution to the problem.

Mark 11:24 The Solution to all of our reception problems. Jesus is telling us to make a choice, a decision... "Therefore, I say unto you whatever things you desire, when you pray believe that you receive them, and you shall have them."

There you have it from the Lord of Lords, The King of Kings, The Author of our Faith, The God Most High. No ifs, and's or buts. Are you telling me pastor is that the reason my daughters cat died is that I didn't believe when I prayed for it?" NO. Jesus is telling you that. I am reporting as ordered.

I challenge each of us to repeat Mark 11:24 out loud at least 3 times a day for the next 30 days. If you accept the challenge your life and the lives of all of your family, team mates, friends and associates will be changed forever.

Stop trying to get more faith, expand your faith, grow your faith or stretch your faith and make a decision to accept the measure of faith you have been given and walk in it. You will be amazed what will happen in your life when you make a conscious decision to believe Jesus and "believe WHEN YOU PRAY that you have received whatever things you desire."

As you ponder these things and pass them on to those you love remember that they are your gift from God. They are the promise reported by Isaiah the prophet from your creator to you. They are "the treasures of darkness and hidden riches of secret places". They have been given to you so that you may know that "I, The Lord, which calleth you by thy name, am the God of Israel". You are the new Israel of whom God speaks. Remember that kings and prophets and wise men sought these things with all that they had and they did not find them. Treasure them in your hearts.

Chapter 4 - Standing On The Promises

Our Precious God is all about love. In His infinite love for us as individuals, He gave us His greatest, most prized possession Jesus, in exchange for our sins.

"For God so greatly loved and dearly prized the world (you, fill in your name) that He even gave up His only begotten Son, so that whoever believes in (trusts in, clings to relies on) Him shall not perish (come to destruction, be lost) but have everlasting life." (John 3:16 Amplified)

Once we accept Jesus as our King and worship Him, we also inherit His great and precious promises. One of which is His faith. We then receive the promises through faith. Yes, we are given the faith of Jesus. How cool is that? We actually have received His faith so that by His faith, we can now receive His promises!

"According to the eternal purpose which He purposed in Jesus our Lord; in whom we have boldness and access with confidence to Him by the faith of Him" (Jesus)!

(Ephesians 3:12 King James Version)

"Knowing that a man is not justified by the works of the law, but BY THE FAITH OF JESUS CHRIST, even we have believed in Jesus Christ, that we might be justified by THE FAITH OF CHRIST, and not by the works of the law; for by the works of the law shall no flesh be justified."

(Galatians 2:16 King James Version)

I am crucified with Christ nevertheless I live; yet not I, but Christ lives in me: and the life which I now live in the flesh, I LIVE BY THE FAITH of the Son of God, who loved me and gave His life for me."

(Galatians 2:20 King James Version)

"Yes doubtless, and I count all things but loss for the excellence of the knowledge of Christ my Lord; for whom I have suffered the loss of all things, and count them as dung, that I may win Christ."

"And be found in Him, not having my own righteousness, which is of the law, but that which is through THE FAITH OF CHRIST, the righteousness which is of God." (Philippians 3:8&9 King James Version)

So, we received His faith when we accepted Him as our King, at which time we were blessed in heavenly places with all spiritual blessings. One of which, is faith:

"Blessed be the God and Father of our Lord Jesus Christ, who hath (past tense) blessed us with all spiritual blessings in heavenly places."

(Ephesians 1:3 King James Version)

PRAISE GOD!!! HERE IS WHY WE SHOULD WAKE UP EVERY MORNING AND LIVE EVERY DAY, LIKE A KID ON CHRISTMAS MORNING! THE PROMISES OF GOD!!!!!

Receive the promises by faith and you will be happy and God will be happy!

Read all about the promises!!!!!

" Simon Peter, a servant and apostle (special messenger) of Jesus Christ To those (whoever accepts Jesus and trusts in relies on and clings to Him) who have (past tense) obtained like precious faith with ourselves in and through the righteousness of our God and Savior Jesus Christ; May grace and peace (which is perfect well being, all necessary good, all spiritual prosperity and freedom from agitating passions and moral conflicts) be multiplied to you in the Knowledge of God and of our Lord Jesus Christ."

"For His divine power has bestowed on us all things that are requisite and suited to life and Godliness, through the full personal knowledge of Him who called us by and to His own glory, and excellence. "By means of these He has bestowed upon us His Precious And Exceedingly Great Promises, So that through them you may escape from the moral decay that is in the world through covetousness and become sharers of the divine nature". (2Peter1: 1-4)

God through Jesus has granted us great and precious promises that give us the desires of our hearts so that we will not have to lust after what other people have. They include but are not limited to: A personal relationship with God and our Lord Jesus, Eternal Life, Faith, Hope, Joy, Positive thinking, Prosperity, Wisdom, Health, Love, Peace, Truth, Kindness, Goodness, Courage, Strength, Happiness, Sanity, Honesty and Gentle Spirits.

The lyrics of the old Gospel song say it all: "Standing on the promises that cannot fail. When the howling storms of doubt and fear assail; by the living word I shall prevail." the evil one and the circumstances of life

When we are attacked by doubt and fear and worry and anxiety and the attacks and lies of appear greater than the unseen to us we stand on the promises of God which will overcome them all.

The promises of God, Can, Not Fail!!! They cannot fail because they are His Word and:

God looks over His Word to perform it!

"Then said the Lord to me, you have seen well, for I am alert and active, looking over My Word to perform it!" (Jeremiah1: 12).

God honors His Word above His Name!

I will worship toward Your holy temple and praise Your name for Your loving-kindness and for Your truth and faithfulness; for You have exalted above all else Your Name and Your Word and You have magnified Your Word above all Your Name!" (Psalm 138:2)

God's Word will not return to Him void!

" For as the rain and snow come down from the heavens and return not there again, but water the earth and make it bring forth and sprout, that it may give seed to the one that sows and bread to the eater, So shall My Word be that goes forth out of My mouth; it shall not return to me void (without producing any effect, useless) but it shall accomplish that which I please and purpose, and it shall prosper in the thing to which I send it." (Isaiah 55:11&12)

God cannot lie!

"God is not a man that He should tell or act a lie, neither is He the son of man that He should feel repentance or compunction. [For what He has promised] Has He said and shall He not do it? Has He spoken and shall not make it good?" (Numbers 23:19)

"Resting in the hope of eternal life, which the ever truthful God Who cannot deceive promised before the world or the ages of time began." (Titus1: 2)

"Accordingly God also, in His desire to show more convincingly and beyond doubt to those who were to inherit the promise the unchangeableness of His purpose and plan, intervened [mediated] with an oath."

" This was so that, by two unchangeable things [His promise and His oath] in which it is impossible for God to prove false or deceive us, we who fled to Him for refuge might have mighty indwelling strength and strong encouragement to grasp and hold fast to the hope appointed for us and set before us." (Hebrews 6:17&18)

God is His Word!

"In the beginning was the Word (Jesus) and the Word was with God and the Word was God Himself"! (John1: 1)

God looks over His Word to perform it. God honors His Word above His name. God's Word will not return to Him void. God cannot lie. God and His Word are the same.

God's promises are His Word. What then are His promises? Research the Word to find them. Here are a few to stand on:

Jesus gave us all of His promises; which are our inheritance and eternal life with only one qualification: That we believe on Him:

Pay Attention! Here Come The Unbreakable Promises of God:

SALVATION!

"Because if you acknowledge and confess with your lips that Jesus is Lord and in your heart believe that God raised Him from the dead you will be saved. For with the heart a person believes and so is justified (found not guilty, declared righteous and acceptable to God) and with the mouth he confesses (declares openly and speaks out freely his faith) and confirms his salvation." (Romans10:9&10)

HEALTH!

Jesus defeated physical and mental disease on the cross. He took the punishment for our sins past, present and future and gave us right standing with God and peace and well- being, in exchange:

"Surely He has borne our griefs (our sicknesses, maladies, infirmities, diseases, weaknesses and distresses and carried our sorrows and pains of punishment, yet we [ignorantly] considered Him stricken and smitten and afflicted by God [as with leprosy]. "

"But He was wounded for our transgressions, He was bruised for our iniquities; the chastisement needful to obtain peace and well being for us was upon Him and by the stripes that wounded Him we are healed and made whole."

(Isaiah 53:4&5)

"He personally bore our sins in His own body on the tree [as on an altar and offered Himself on it], that we might die (cease to exist) to sin and live by righteousness. By His wounds you have been healed."

(1 Peter 2:24)

"And these signs shall accompany those who believe: They shall lay hands on the sick and the sick will get well"

(Mark 16:17&18)

ABUNDANT LIFE (PROSPERITY)

"The thief comes only in order to steal and kill and destroy. I came that they may have and enjoy life and have it in abundance (to the full till it overflows)."

(John 10:10)

" For you are becoming progressively acquainted with and recognizing more strongly and clearly the grace of our Lord Jesus Christ (His kind ness, His gracious generosity, His undeserved favor and spiritual blessing) in that though He was so very rich, He became so very poor, in order that by His poverty you might become enriched (abundantly supplied)."

(2Corinthians 8:9)

POWER AND AUTHORITY OVER satan!

Jesus promised us and gave us dominion over satan and all of his powers and authority. Jesus declared that as His faithful believers; nothing shall in anywise harm us:

" And He said to them", "I saw satan falling like a lightning flash from heaven." {Jesus saw satan fall from heaven like a lightning flash because Jesus threw him.}

"Behold, I have given you (fill in your name) authority and power to trample serpents and scorpions (not snakes and scorpions but the minions, demons and soldiers of the evil one) and physical and mental strength and ability over all the powers that the enemy possesses; and nothing shall in anywise harm you."

(Luke 10:18&19)

We have been given the power and responsibility to bind satan on earth and in heaven and to drive out his demons.

"Truly I say to you, whatever you bind on earth is bound in heaven and whatever you loose on earth shall be loosed in heaven." (Matthew 18:19 King James Version)

"And these signs will accompany those who believe: in My name they shall drive out demons; They will speak in new languages; They will pick up serpents; and if they drink any deadly thing it shall not harm them (not snakes and poison but the strongest powers of the evil one), they will lay hands on the sick and the sick will get well."

(Mark 16:17&18)

JESUS' POWER AND STRENGTH AND ABILITY TO WORK MIRACLES!

Jesus promised us His power and strength and that He will give us whatever we ask in His Name:

"I assure you most solemnly I tell you, if anyone steadfastly believes on Me; the works that I do shall he do also and even greater than these shall he do because I go to My Father."

"And I will do [I myself will grant]; whatever you ask in My name [as presenting all that I AM] so that the Father may be glorified in the Son. Yes, I will grant [I myself will do for you] whatever you shall ask in My Name [as presenting all that I AM]."

(John 14:12-14)

Jesus promised that we would ask what we wish and it will be done for us:

ANSWERED PRAYER AND GRANTED WISHES!

"If you live in Me [abide vitally united to Me] and My Words remain in you and continue to live in your hearts, ask what you wish and it shall be done unto you."

(John 15:7)

"Until now you have not asked a single thing in My Name but now ask and keep on asking and you will receive that your joy may be full and complete."

(John 16: 24)

"Keep on asking and it will be given you; keep on knocking and the door will be opened to you. For everyone that keeps on asking receives and he who keeps on seeking finds; and to him who keeps on knocking the door will be opened.

"Or what man is there of you, if his son asks him for a loaf of bread, will hand him a stone? Or if he asks for a fish, will hand him a serpent?"

" If you then, being evil know how to give good and advantageous gifts to your children, how much more will your Father in heaven [perfect as He is] give good and advantageous gifts to those who keep on asking Him?"

(Matthew 7:7)

THE POWER TO SPEAK AND RECEIVE!

Jesus promised that: we will have what we say as long as we have no doubt or unbelief:

"Truly I tell you whoever says to this mountain, be lifted up and thrown into the sea! And does not doubt in his heart but believes that what he says will take place it will be done for him. For this reason I am telling you whatever you ask for in prayer, believe (trust and be confident) that it is granted to you, and you will get it." (Mark 11:22&23)

THE POWER OF AGREEMENT!

Jesus promised that whenever two of us agree about anything, it shall be done for us and that when two or more of us are gathered in His name, there He is in the middle of us:

"Again I tell you, if two of you on earth agree (harmonize together as making a symphony together) about whatever [anything and everything] they may ask, it will come to pass and be done for them by My Father in heaven." Matthew 18:19

HIS PRESENCE WITH US!

"For whenever two or three are gathered (drawn together as My followers) in My name, there I AM in the midst of them".

(Matthew 18:19&20)

"And behold, I am with you all the days to the very consumption of the age." (Matthew 28:20)

ANGELIC PROTECTION AND THE ABILITY TO ASSIGN ANGELS

"For He will give His angels charge over you to accompany and defend and preserve you in all your ways!"

(Psalm 91:11)

"I assure you, most solemnly I tell you if anyone steadfastly believes in Me, he will himself be able to do the things that I do and; and he will do even greater than these, because I go to My Father"

(John 14:12)

" Do you suppose that I cannot appeal to My Father, and He will immediately provide Me with more than twelve legions [more than 80,000] of angels?"

(Matthew 26:53)

"Are not the angels all ministering spirits (servants) sent out in the service [of God for the assistance] of those who are to inherit salvation?

(Hebrews 1:14)

ALL THINGS NECESSARY TO LIFE AND GODLINESS!

"For His divine power has bestowed upon us all things that [are requisite and suited] to life and Godliness, through the full personal knowledge of Him Who called us by and to His own glory and excellence."

(2Peter1:3)

That scripture sums it all up. God has promised and delivered to us everything we need to live powerful, healthy and prosperous life. We receive all of the promises by faith. He even gave us His faith to employ.

Believe and Receive and let your joy be full!

STAND ON THE PROMISES OF GOD!

Ingest the truth! What great words of faith proclaimed by John Hood, the writer. Read the Words of Jesus: "It is the Spirit that brings life. The flesh conveys no benefits at all; there is no profit in it. The Words (truths) that I have been speaking to you are Spirit and Life." (John 6:63)

Surely we overcome doubt and fear by standing on the promises that; cannot fail. Why, because the promises are Spirit and Life. They make alive, and they are eternal truth. The Words of Jesus are of the Spirit and are eternal. Doubt and unbelief are of the flesh.

Chapter 5 – Why are You So Fearful?

Do you ever consider Jesus' feelings? What a weird way to start a teaching about overcoming fear. But it is, a valid question. It is very unusual to think about Jesus' feelings. Usually, my thoughts are centered on my feelings and rarely if ever on His. Isn't that strange? He loved us so much that He gave His life in a very humiliating and painful death. He guaranteed our inheritances and the great and precious promises of His Gospel, with His blood. Yet, we rarely ask ourselves how He may feel.

Consider this writing from our appointed teacher, Paul:

"Seeing then that we have a great high priest, that is passed into the heavens, Jesus the Son of God, let us hold fast our profession. For WE HAVE NOT AN HIGH PRIEST WHICH CANNOT BE TOUCHED WITH THE FEELING OF OUR INFIRMITIES (weaknesses); But was in all points tempted like as we are, yet without sin. Let us then come boldly TO THE THRONE OF GRACE that we may obtain mercy, and find grace to help in time of need." (Hebrews 4:15&16)

And the shortest verse in the Bible reported by the disciple John; an eyewitness to the fact, about Jesus' reaction to the unbelief of His closest friends:

"JESUS WEPT". (John 11:35)

We all have hurt His feelings. Unbelief is the surest way to do so. Consider two true eyewitness news accounts of colossal levels of unbelief, which surely must have made Jesus weep.

The following event was reported almost identically by two eyewitnesses: John and Matthew, and by the greatest news reporter who ever lived, Dr. Luke. Luke personally interviewed and reported precisely, the eyewitness accounts of hundreds of people who were present at the time of Jesus.

The scene is at the Jordan river, where John the baptist is prophesying the coming of Jesus.

He is preparing the way for the coming of the Messiah by baptizing. Jesus has come to be baptized also.

"And Jesus, when He was baptized, went up straightway out of the water: and lo, THE HEAVENS WERE OPENED UP UNTO HIM, AND HE SAW THE SPIRIT OF GOD DESCENDING LIKE A DOVE, AND LIGHTING UPON HIM: AND LO, A VOICE FROM HEAVEN SAYING, THIS IS MY SON IN WHOM, I AM WELL PLEASED." (Matthew 3:16&17)

"Now when all the people were baptized, it came to pass, that Jesus being also baptized and praying, THE HEAVEN WAS OPENED, AND THE HOLY GHOST DESCENDED IN A BODILY

SHAPE AS A DOVE UPON HIM, AND A VOICE CAME FROM HEAVEN SAYING..... THOU

ART MY BELOVED SON; IN THEE, AM I WELL PLEASED." (Luke 3:21 &22)

"And John (John the disciple is writing about John the Baptist) bare record, saying, I SAW THE SPIRIT DESCENDING FROM HEAVEN LIKE A DOVE, AND IT ABODE UPON HIM. And I knew Him not but He that sent me to baptize with water, the same said unto me, UPON WHOM THOU SHALT SEE THE SPIRIT DESCENDING, AND REMAINING ON HIM, THE SAME IS HE WHICH BAPTIZETH WITH THE HOLY GHOST AND I SAW HIM, AND BARE RECORD THAT THIS IS THE SON OF GOD." (John 1:32-34)

Thus, it is recorded clearly three times that John the Baptist got first hand visual and audible confirmation directly from GOD that JESUS was HIS SON.

Jesus spoke of John the Baptist: "FOR I SAY UNTO YOU, AMONG THOSE THAT ARE BORN OF WOMEN THERE IS NOT A GREATER PROPHET THAN JOHN THE BAPTIST: but he that is least in the kingdom is greater than he." (Luke 7:28)

Now, Jesus himself has proclaimed that until Jesus, John the Baptist was the Greatest Prophet Who Ever Lived. Yet, when faced with the certainty of his execution for condemning King Herod, John was overcome by unbelief.

"And it came to pass, that when Jesus had made an end of commanding his twelve disciples, He departed thence to teach and to preach in their cities. Now when John had heard in the prison the works of Christ, he sent two of his (John's) disciples, And said unto Him (Jesus)..... ART THOU HE THAT SHOULD COME, OR DO WE LOOK FOR ANOTHER?"

Jesus answered and said unto them, GO AND SHOW JOHN AGAIN THOSE THINGS WHICH YOU DO HEAR AND SEE: THE BLIND RECEIVE THEIR SIGHT, AND THE LAME WALK, THE LEPERS ARE CLEANSED, AND THE DEAF HEAR, THE DEAD ARE RAISED UP, AND THE POOR HAVE THE GOSPEL PREACHED TO THEM, AND BLESSED IS HE WHO WILL NOT BE OFFENDED IN ME." (Matthew 11:1 -6)

Is the evil one good at deceit? Don't you know that he was buzzing in John's ear that Jesus could save him if He wanted to. Imagine all of the trash that the evil one tempted John with.

John KNEW WHO JESUS WAS! GOD DECLARED IN A HEAVENLY AND AUDIBLE VOICE TO JOHN, WHOM JESUS WAS! Yet, fear overcame the certain knowledge of JESUS.

You would think that the disciples, who personally witnessed all of the above as well as Jesus feeding 5000 men not including women and children from three loaves and two fishes, would use more belief. Yet, read on:

This event took place IMMEDIATELY after the feeding of the thousands. The disciples had fed all of the throng and still collected 12 baskets of remnants. One full basket for each disciple:

And when they had sent away the multitude, they took Him even as He was in the ship And there were other little ships. AND THERE AROSE A GREAT STORM OF WIND, AND THE WAVES BEAT THE SHIP, SO THAT IT WAS NOW FULL. AND HE WAS IN THE HINDER PART OF THE SHIP, ASLEEP ON A PILLOW; AND THEY WOKE HIM AND SAID

UNTO HIM,..... MASTER, CAREST NOT THAT WE PERISH?

AND HE AROSE, AND REBUKED THE WIND, AND SAID UNTO THE SEA, ...PEACE, BE STILL. AND THE WIND CEASED AND THERE WAS A GREAT CALM....
AND HE SAID UNTO THEM,.....WHY ARE YOU SO

FEARFUL?.....
HOW IS IT THAT YOU HAVE NO FAITH?

And they feared exceedingly, and said one to another, What manner of man is this, that even the wind and the sea obey him?" (Mark 4:37-40)

The questions are the most important part of this teaching:

(1) "WHY ARE YOU SO FEARFUL?"

(2) "HOW IS IT THAT YOU HAVE NO FAITH?"

The first question is the most pertinent to us. The second is not possible for Christians to claim now. Since we receive the free gift of "the measure of faith" when we are saved, we do not have the excuse that we had to rely on our flesh faith, and it failed us. (Ephesians 2:8&9 and Romans 12:3)

Using our faith is a choice that we make and belief is a decision. The burning question remains, "WHY ARE YOU SO FEARFUL?" The answer is obvious. Unbelief. Remember Jesus' reply to John the Baptist:

"Go and show John again those things which you do see: The blind receive sight, and the lame walk, the lepers are cleansed, and the deaf hear, the dead are raised up, and the poor have the gospel preached to them."

"And blessed is he whosoever is not offended in me."

Jesus answered John's question about His deity by reminding him of specific fulfilled prophecy:

"And in that day, shall the deaf hear the words of the book, and the eyes of the blind shall see out of obscurity, and out of the darkness." (Isaiah 29:18)

"Then the eyes of the blind shall be opened, and the ears of the deaf shall be unstopped. Then shall the lame man leap as a dear, and the tongue of the dumb sing: for in the wilderness shall waters break out, and streams in the dessert." (Isaiah 35:5&6)

"The Spirit of the Lord is upon me; for He has anointed me to preach the good news of the gospel to the poor, He has sent me to bind up the broken hearted, to proclaim liberty to the captives and the opening of the prison to them that are bound; To proclaim the acceptable year of the Lord, and the day of vengeance of our God; to comfort all that mourn."

"To appoint unto them that mourn in Zion, to give unto them beauty for ashes, the oil of joy for mourning, the garment of praise for the spirit of heaviness that they might be called trees of righteousness, the planting of the Lord, that He might be glorified." (Isaiah 61:1)

Then Jesus sent the following second message to John... "And blessed is he who takes no offense at Me and finds no cause for stumbling in or through Me and is not hindered from seeing the TRUTH." (Matthew 11:6 Amplified Bible)

Jesus' question to the disciples is more appropriately asked of us in this form: HOW IS IT THAT YOU CHOOSE NOT TO USE THE FAITH (making a decision to live one moment at a time, with joyful expectation of the things that we cannot see) THAT I HAVE GIVEN YOU AS A FREE GIFT?

Does it seem odd that the disciples asked the creator of the winds and the waves if He cared that they perished? Does it seem even more strange that they were shocked that the winds and the waves obeyed Him? Are we different?

Jesus clearly is saying to us as well as He did to them, that the way to overcome fear, is to remember who He is, and what He promised. And, to choose to use the free gift of faith that we have been given. His faith.

We all have storms in our lives. Jesus taught us how to overcome them. Fear is not the answer. As a matter of fact, Jesus commanded us not to worry. If you have trouble overcoming worry, read Matthew 6:25-34 five times a day for three months. I guarantee you that you will change.

Meditate on this teaching from Jesus:

"VERILY, VERILY I SAY UNTO YOU, HE THAT BELIEVETH ON ME, THE WORKS THAT I DO SHALL HE DO ALSO; AND GREATER THAN THESE SHALL HE DO; BECAUSE I GO TO MY FATHER." (John 14:12)

The works that He did, we shall do also, if we believe on Him. What did Jesus do in the storm?

He spoke to it!

"PEACE ... BE STILL"

I pray that this teaching has blessed you. If you have been blessed, please pass it to another who will be blessed.

Are you fearful? Speak to the storm in your life and command it... "Peace Be Still"

Chapter 6 – Worried?

There is no temptation but that which is common to all people. Are you worried? Ask yourself this question, have you ever allowed your Monday to ruin your Sunday? Do you hate the thought of Monday? Are there mountains in your life that you believe in your heart are insurmountable? Have you lost sleep recently because of a financial challenge or a health problem, or the fear of losing your job, or the fear of losing your business, or the fear of losing your relationship, or the fear of what tomorrow may bring, or the fear of fear, or the fear of what people think about you, or the fear of the power of the evil one, or the fear that God has removed his hand of protection from you, or the fear that even though God has heard your prayer he may not answer it for whatever reasons including your performance, or the fear of another person's problems. Do any of these things seem hopeless? Do you feel like there is no solution to the point that you worry? Do you ever just have a moment of honesty and speak that you are worried?

I want to share an amazing true testimony with you. About three years ago, a man came to me for help. He came to me largely because he had worn out all of the other counselors and ministers in his life. This man is a very learned man. He is also a very nice man. At this time in his life. He was so worried and anxious that he was in a constant state of despair. Eventually, he became so tired of being worried that he became willing to do almost anything. We had several sessions that lasted for at least two hours. It seemed that we were getting nowhere. The one thing that kept me engaged in trying to help this man was his willingness to try.

Finally, I told my friend to read the following scripture three times a day for 90 days, until he had it memorized and could quote every jot and title of it. After 60 days he began to change and very shortly his life and his outlook on life turned 180 degrees and he is a new person. Anxiety and Worry have left him. This man is almost unrecognizable as the same person. Here is the scripture that he read out loud three times a day for thirty days...If you will do this, your life will never be the same.

Matthew 6:25-34.... A teaching from our Lord and Savior...The creator of all things...

"Therefore I say to you, do not worry about your life, what you will eat or what you will drink; nor about your body, what you will put on. Is not life more than food and the body more than clothing?" "Look at the birds of the air, for they neither sow nor reap nor gather into barns; yet your heavenly Father feeds them. Are you not of more value than they?"

"Which of you by worrying can add one cubit to his stature?"

"So why do you worry about clothing? Consider the lilies of the field, how they grow; they neither toil nor spin; and yet I say to you that even Solomon in all his glory was not arrayed like one of these."

" Now if God so clothes the grass of the field, which today is here and tomorrow is thrown into the oven, will He not much more clothe you, oh you of little faith? "

"Therefore do not worry, saying, what shall we eat? Or what shall we drink? Or what shall we wear? For all these things the Gentiles seek. For your heavenly Father knows that you need all these things."

"But seek ye first the kingdom of God (Jesus) and His righteousness (His righteousness, not yours), and all these things shall be added to you."

"Therefore, do not worry about tomorrow, for tomorrow will worry about tomorrow, for tomorrow will worry about its own things. Sufficient for the day is its own troubles."

Note that Jesus repeats his commandment not suggestion "Do Not Worry" three times in this teaching.

Back to our friend who repeated this teaching three times a day out loud for 90 days... about one year after the word of God transformed him into a new person, he came to me and asked that we agree in prayer for a powerful and immediate conversion experience for his son who was lost and in the full blown service of

Satan. He was very concerned about his son but he had made a decision to trust Jesus and not worry any more. About three weeks later if I remember correctly, His son had a profound salvation experience and is one of the coolest Jesus freaks I know. He spends most of his time studying the Word and teaching it and helping his friends who need Jesus.

At a recent meeting, his Son told me that if he had not seen the profound change in his Dad that," He (his Dad) could never have led me to the Lord."

# #

Chapter 7 – Anxious?

Several of you have related to me recently some attacks of anxiety. I have also been tempted with this old trick of the evil one. Anxiety can evolve from tension or nervousness to fear to paralysis to a persistent feeling of unknown or known impending doom.

Note how the evil one perpetrates this trick on us over and over again. In AA meetings you will hear FEAR treated as an acronym F.E.A.R. = False, Events, Appearing, Real. The devil is but a liar. He is the father of all lies. He will lie to us until we fight back by telling him to shut up while making a decision to believe. Once we make a decision to believe Jesus there is no reason for fear.

Think about God's message sent through his messengers to us. Every time Jesus or angels appear, the first thing they say to us is "Fear not". Ask yourself why.

Are you anxious? Jesus gave me a message recently to give to all of the team members of one of our partners that I would like to share with you. The message is from the fourth chapter of Paul the teacher to the gentiles[1] letter to the church at Philippi. It was revealed to him by the Holy Spirit. It is not a judgment. It is a wonderful promise.

"Be anxious for nothing". Remember that to be anxious for nothing is a moment by moment decision, "but in all things through prayer and supplication... (surrendering your flesh. Understanding that it is not about you. Making a decision to believe the promises of Jesus. Asking and therefore knowing that you receive when you ask...Mark 11:24) "With thanksgiving in your heart"...this is a powerful directive. We have thanksgiving in our heart because we have made the decision to believe that we have received from our Father who said that he will give us anything if we ask and that he has already given us all things that pertain to life and Godliness.

"Let your requests be known to God". We are to ask for whatever the desires of our hearts are. We have been taught that it is greedy to ask for things for ourselves. WRONG! We are to ask that we may receive. Here are a few of the promises of Jesus that when you speak them will cause commotion among works oriented folk.
"Until now you have asked nothing, ask that you may receive that your joy may be full".

"If you being evil know how to give good gifts to your children, how much more will your heavenly Father give you good things if you ask?"

"Ask anything in my name and I will give it to you"

"Whenever two or more of you agree touching anything in the earth, asking anything of the Father in the name of the Son, it shall be given to you."

"Ask the Father anything in the name of the Son and it shall be given you that the Father may be glorified through the son".

"Therefore, I tell you, whatsoever things you desire, when you pray believe that you receive and they shall be yours".

Continuing Paul's teaching…"and the peace that passes all understanding will guard your hearts and minds in Jesus."

Think about it this way:

1. Commandment… "Be Anxious for nothing".

2. Directions for how to obey the commandment…"

In ALL things…through prayer and supplication" again this means surrendering our will, making a decision to believe the seen more than the unseen; not to deal with the situation, problem or challenge in our minds or flesh.

"With thanksgiving in our hearts...as earlier, make a decision to believe that because of our reconciled position with God, we have been given all things that pertain to life and Godliness. Make a decision to believe that Jesus meant what he said in the promises you just read. Making a decision to believe Jesus will cause a spirit of thanksgiving to come over us. Thanksgiving is evidence of a decision to believe.

3. Promise of reward for obeying the commandment,

"and the peace that passes all understanding will guard your hearts and minds in Jesus." I have counseled literally thousands of people in all walks of life and I assure you that the thing that people desire more than any other thing is peace. Right here the Bible shows us how to receive the thing we want most in life and it is this simple, MAKE A DECISION TO BE ANXIOUS FOR NOTHING.

There is a huge power promise to the receipt of peace. Your hearts and minds will be guarded by Jesus. WOW! This is a huge teaching. I promise not to go off to deep on this teaching right now, but trust me you could write a novel about this one promise.

Why do your heart and mind need guarding? Because from the overflow of your heart your mouth will speak. What you believe in your heart you will speak without doubt from your mouth and you can and most assuredly will have what you say, if it is said without doubt.

As you set the course of this moment, I pray and believe that this teaching will bless and keep you on the narrow path with Jesus.

Chapter 8 - In God's Time

Have you ever heard the old cliché teachings about, "**In God's Time**"? The inference being that God answers our prayers when he gets around to it or when he is motivated by some unreported standard of performance on our part.

I have received reports of many in our flock who have been taught that," God's time is not our time and that he will answer our prayers in his time. I have been taught this myself. Worse, I actually know people who believe this, in spite of the fact that it is not Biblical. **That is why I recently published a teaching on "God's Time". The fact is that God's Time is the speed of thought and is in this present moment.**

Here is a scripture about God's time that you will find very interesting.

From the book of John chapter 6 beginning in verse 14...

"Then those men, when they had seen the miracle that Jesus did, said, this is of a truth that prophet that should come into the world. When Jesus therefore perceived that they would come and take him by force, to make him a king, he departed again into a mountain himself alone.

73

And when night was come, his disciples went down unto the sea, And entered into a ship, and went over the sea toward Capernaum, And it was now dark, and Jesus was not come to them. And the sea arose by the reason of a great wind that blew.

So, when they had rowed about five and twenty or thirty furlongs, they saw Jesus walking on the sea and drawing nigh unto the ship; and they were afraid. But he saith unto them, It is I; be not afraid. Then they willingly received him into the ship and IMMEDIATELY THE SHIP WAS AT THE LAND WHITHER THEY WENT."

Please note that Jesus caused the ship to IMMEDIATELY be at the land whither they went. As you ponder "God's time", consider the word IMMEDIATELY. Watch the reaction to this from the people. Verse 22, continues...

"The day following when the people which stood on the other side of the sea saw that there was none other boats there, save that one where into his disciples were entered, and that Jesus went not with his disciples in the boat, but that his disciples were gone away alone;

{Howbeit there came other boats from Tiberius nigh unto the place where they did eat bread; after that the Lord gave thanks;} (This is referring to the fact that this teaching began with Jesus feeding the five thousand not including women and children and had given thanks to the Lord.)

When the people therefore saw that Jesus was not there, neither his disciples, they also took shipping and came to Capernaum, seeking for Jesus. And when they had found him on the other side of the sea, they said unto him, Rabbi, WHEN CAMEST THOU HITHER?" (In other words, how did you get here?...IMMEDIATELY...at the speed of thought?)

Here is another "Jesus' Speed" teaching. If you think these teachings of Jesus' make stiff necked religious people angry now, think how angry they made the Hebrews who were being taught that everything that they had been taught was about HIM, and not them. Jesus had just finished reading the scroll of Isaiah 61 out loud in the temple. He proclaimed that this prophecy was about him. "The Spirit of the Lord is upon me, because he hath anointed me to preach the gospel to the poor; he hath sent me to heal the brokenhearted, to preach deliverance to the captives, and recovering of sight to the blind, to set at liberty them that are bruised, To preach the acceptable year of the Lord." And he closed the book, and he gave it again to the minister, and sat down, And the eyes of all them that were in the synagogue were fastened on him, and he began to say unto them, "This day is this scripture fulfilled in your ears."

Then the people said....Hey wait a minute we know this guy, he's Josephs son, we know his brothers and sisters and his Mother. So Jesus tells them that no prophet is accepted in his own country and rebukes them for their unbelief. He tells them that they are going to be condemned worse than Sodom and Tyre.

Beginning again from the 28th verse of Luke chapter 4...

"And all they in the synagogue when they heard these things, were filled with wrath, and rose up, and thrust him out of the city, and led him out of the city, and led him unto the brow of the hill whereon their city, was built that they might cast him down headlong. BUT HE PASSING THROUGH THE MIDST OF THEM WENT HIS WAY. Get this...He passed right through them...How Did He Pass Right Through Them? IMMEDIATELY? At the speed of thought?

Chapter 9 – Our Daily Bread

A great multitude of people followed Jesus from all of the area surrounding Jerusalem. They came from Galilee and Decapolis and from beyond Jordan on foot to hear God in the person of Jesus teach them. Jesus went up into a mountain and He spoke to the assembled, teaching them and us, how to live a blessed life.

We know the beginning of his teaching as "The Beatitudes". You have heard these in Church. They begin..." Blessed are the poor in spirit (those whose egos are contained well enough to make them teachable) for theirs is the Kingdom of Heaven. Jesus is teaching as the voice of God the Father come to earth in the flesh to tell us how we should live. In this teaching reported by Matthew beginning in the 5th chapter, there are contained many of the best known and most frequently quoted, teachings of Jesus.

While he is directing us in the various areas of life, Jesus explains how we are to communicate with Him in prayer. We find this teaching beginning in the 6th chapter of Matthew and the 7th verse.

"But when you pray, use not vain repetitions, as do the heathens (those who worship other gods) do; for they think that they shall be heard for their much speaking. Be not ye therefore like unto them; FOR YOUR FATHER KNOWETH WHAT THINGS YE HAVE NEED OF BEFORE YE ASK HIM.

After this manner therefore pray ye;

Our Father which art in Heaven,
Hallowed be thy name.
Thy Kingdom come,
Thy will be done on earth,
As it is in heaven.

GIVE US THIS DAY OUR DAILY BREAD!

And forgive us our debts as we forgive our debtors.
And lead us not into temptation, but deliver us from evil;
For thine is the kingdom, and the power and the glory,
forever. Amen."

How many times have we prayed this prayer? It is prayed at civic group meetings, in churches, in AA and all 12 step related meetings and in homes all around the world every day. Most people can quote this the "Lord's Prayer" verbatim.

How many times have we blown right past this simple line that is the essence of our communication with God? Remember that the teacher is Jesus acting as God in the flesh come to earth to teach us how to communicate with him in prayer.

Jesus teaches us to ask our Heavenly Father the one who created us and all things to.

"Give us this day our daily bread!'

Please note that Jesus did not teach us to pray saying:

Give us this day our daily bread... In your time.

Give us this day our daily bread... When we pass the test.

Give us this day our daily bread... Unless we are planning to consume it on our own lusts.

Give us this day our daily bread... When we complete the process that you are taking us through to prepare us to receive the bread.

Give us this day our daily bread... If it be thy will.

Give us this day our daily bread... unless it will harm us.

Give us this day our daily bread... If we have first prayed for everyone else.

Give us this day our daily bread... If we are in right standing with you.

Give us this day our daily bread... if you are not upset with us about what we did yesterday.

Please note that Jesus is teaching us to believe that we receive when we pray:

"GIVE US THIS DAY, OUR DAILY BREAD"!

Jesus confirmed this teaching as reported by Mark in the 11th Chapter and the 24th verse.

"Therefore I say unto you, what things soever ye desire, when ye pray, BELIEVE that you receive them and you shall have them."

I frequently ask for a show of hands when I preach, of those who are believing God "FOR" things. This is a common mis-teaching in the church today. We have been taught to believe, "FOR" things. This belief is usually stated as..."I am believing God for that big deal that I've been standing in faith for."" I know that God is going to...so and so and so and so." "I am believing God for my healing."

This incorrect belief permanently postpones our blessings. If you believe "FOR" something you are postponing that thing. This belief system originates with unbelief, fear or ignorance of the teachings of Jesus. It is a way of explaining away why you did not receive a thing that you prayed for. The question would be stated, "Pastor, I prayed for the big deal/healing/ money etc. and I did not get it. Please explain."

The correct answer is that you received whatever you requested when you prayed and asked for it. It was given to you at the moment you accepted Jesus as your Lord and Savior. You may not see it with your natural eye, but we do not fix our eyes on the things that are seen, but the things that are unseen, for the seen is temporal and subject to change; but the unseen is eternal. We receive when we believe without seeing and live in this present moment with joyful expectation that we have already been given all things that pertain to life and Godliness.

If you are confused, don't feel alone. The wisdom of God is foolishness to man and the wisdom of man is foolishness to God. Many teachers are also confused. That is why they try to explain away the truth by making up excuses for God. Such as..." You don't have enough faith". This is a very common mis-teaching. The truth is that at the moment you accepted Jesus as your Lord you got His faith...the full measure of faith. You will never get more faith than, The Faith of The Son of God." (Romans 12:3, Ephesians 2:8 and 9, Ephesians 2:20)

Jesus came to earth and gave us a simple and effective prescription for joy, peace and abundance in this life and in the life to come. Consider again His commandment from Matthew chapter 6 verse 34...

"Take therefore no thought for the morrow; for the morrow shall take thought for the things of itself. Sufficient unto the day is the evil thereof."

Jesus is asking us to ask today for our daily bread and believe that when we pray, we receive, whether or not we see. Try his prescription you have been blessed.

Chapter 10 - Do You Need The Power Of God?

At this point in His earth walk, many thousands of people were following Jesus and the crowds were growing daily. On one particular day as the sun began to set, Jesus perceived their physical hunger. Most of us know the report of what happened next.

Jesus knowing what he would do, asked his disciple Phillip, "Whence shall we buy bread, that these may eat?" Phillip answered Jesus and said that it would take nearly a years wages to buy enough bread to feed the people. Then Peters brother Andrew said to Jesus that there was a boy in the crowd that had 5 loaves and 2 small fish. Then Andrew asked Jesus, "but what are they among so many?" And Jesus said, "Make them sit down."

Now there were about five thousand men, not including women and children. And Jesus took the loaves; and when he had given thanks, he distributed to the disciples, and the disciples to the crowd. And the crowd ate as much as they wanted. When they were filled, He said unto His disciples, "Gather up the fragments that remain, that nothing be lost."

The disciples gathered the fragments and filled twelve baskets. Note that: there were twelve baskets left over. One basket for each disciple. All of this from 5 loaves and 2 small fish.

What happened next is not surprising. "Then those men said, This is of a truth that prophet that should come into the world." Then they started trying to capture Jesus to make Him their king. Jesus did not wish to be their king and He escaped and went into a mountain to pray. When night came, His disciples got into their boat to go across the sea to go to Capernaum. A storm rose up and the men were afraid as the small boat was being tossed about. This must have been quite a storm because many of the disciples were fishermen and lived on the sea.

Jesus appeared to them walking on the sea. Jesus instructed them not to be afraid and entered into the boat and IMMEDIATELY, the boat was at the land that they were going to.

The crowd that saw the miracle of Jesus feeding the thousands, chased the disciples across the lake to try to catch Him. They knew that He had not left with the disciples and they were shocked to find Him with them. They asked Jesus how He got there.

Now Jesus teaches us all a lesson of great power. "Verily, verily, I say unto you, Ye seek me not because ye saw the miracles, but because ye did eat of the loaves and were filled." "Labor not for the meat which perishes, but for that meat which endureth unto everlasting life, which the son of man shall give unto you; for Him hath God the Father sealed." In other words, do not seek a temporary solution to a permanent problem. They got fed physical food and wanted another free meal for their stomachs. Jesus is saying, accept me and you will have your daily food and a life time of blessings in this life and the life to come.

What is the meat that endureth unto everlasting life that Jesus gave us? Read on.

Jesus immediately announced the key to God and Heaven. Jesus explains the NEW COVENANT. Here is the answer to the mystery of the ages. This is the question that men have always asked God and are still asking Him, even though Jesus came to earth as God in the flesh to answer the question without ambiguity. Here is the deal with God that is so simple that no one can claim confusion or the inability to understand, yet most refuse to accept or believe it.

Then they said unto Him, "what shall we do that we might do the works of God?" In plain language, they are asking, what is the deal with God? Do we have to keep all of the commandments? Do we have to be good? Do we have to be perfect or just really good? Which commandments are more important than others?" Is adultery worse than murder? Is gossip and judgment ok but fornication is not?" Is pride a worse sin than stealing?" How good on a scale of one to ten do I have to be to get God to bless me or let me into heaven?" Do good people go to heaven and bad people go to hell?" "What do we have to do to close the deal with God?" "What do we have to do to get God to like us enough to bless us?"

Here is the answer out of the mouth of God in the flesh come to earth in the person of Jesus.

"THIS IS THE WORK OF GOD, THAT YOU BELIEVE ON HIM WHOM HE HATH SENT!

What is the meat that endureth unto everlasting life that Jesus gave us? Read on.

Jesus continues in this teaching about Power and eternal life and the NEW COVENANT. The Hebrews have told Jesus that they are under Moses and the Mosaic covenant. Jesus is telling them that the program has changed and that He is the new deal sent from God. They tell Jesus that Moses provided manna for them in the wilderness. They cling to the old covenant of works and law and Jesus explains clearly that there is a new deal with God and that He is it. The discussion about bread comes from the tribes of Israel being condemned to wander in the wilderness for 40 years because they refused to believe God and they rejected him. During their nomadic wandering, God caused manna which we know as bread to come down from the sky to feed them.

"Your fathers did eat manna in the wilderness and are dead. (Later that day Jesus asks this question, Did not Moses give you the law, Yet NONE of you keep it? To keep the commandments is impossible for a man to do) This is the bread which cometh down from heaven, that a man may eat thereof, and not die. I am the living bread which came down from heaven: If any man eats of this bread he shall live for ever; and the bread that I will give is my flesh which I will give for the life of the world." (Jesus is teaching that His flesh will be given not just for the Hebrews, but for the Non-Hebrews or gentiles, who at this time were lost and without hope in the world and were not candidates for salvation.)

"Verily, verily I say unto you, Except you eat the flesh of the Son of man, and drink his blood, you have no life in you."

(Jesus is saying that if we do not accept the new deal which is to believe on Him and accept His blood as the key to the new covenant, then we are on our own, that we then must justify ourselves to God by our performance which is not possible. Jesus is saying that His blood and His gospel are the new covenant. He is stating clearly that our relationship with God is based on What Jesus did not what we do.)

"Whoso eateth My flesh and drinketh my blood, hath eternal life; and I will raise him up at the last day, FOR MY FLESH IS MEAT INDEED AND MY BLOOD IS DRINK INDEED. HE THAT EATETH MY FLESH (consumes my Words and believes them) AND DRINKETH MY BLOOD (Accepts that my blood paid the price in full for their relationship with God) DWELLETH IN ME AND I IN HIM." This is the essence of the Gospel of Jesus. All he is asking is that we make a decision not to be Self-Reliant and accept Him and His complete work as our conduit to God. He is promising that if we make this decision that He will live in us, and we will live in Him. If we have Jesus living in us and we are living in Him, what would we be lacking?

So, what is the meat that endureth unto everlasting life that Jesus gave us? Read on.

At this point the disciples freak completely. They now know that Jesus is saying that He has replaced the old covenant, the Ten Commandments and the 600 ordinances that followed and the entire Levitical priest organization attached, with His blood. They know that this will cause the Pharisees and the Sadducees that live by keeping God's people under the bondage of the law and their performance, to want to kill them all.

They begin to think and ask in their minds, which Jesus reads..."are you sure about this Jesus? you are overturning the whole program and you are going to get us murdered".

Read Jesus' reply..."Doth this offend you?" " What and if ye shall see the Son of man ascend up where he was before?" Jesus did ascend into the clouds right in front of the very men of whom he asked this question. This was to fulfill the prophetic question that he had just asked and to remove any doubt that He spoke the truth.

Jesus is about to explain what the meat that endureth unto everlasting life is. "It is the Spirit that quickeneth (makes alive); the flesh profiteth nothing; THE WORDS THAT I SPEAK UNTO YOU ARE SPIRIT AND ARE LIFE." "BUT THERE ARE SOME OF YOU THAT BELIEVE NOT."

Jesus has just explained what the meat that endureth forever is, HIS WORDS! Then in an amazing crescendo, Jesus explains the entire problem over which He has no power then or now; "BUT THERE ARE SOME AMONG YOU WHO DO NOT BELIEVE." Obviously Jesus knows that belief and unbelief are free will choices that we make. We may choose to believe or we may choose to not believe, Jesus can not and never will take away this choice from us.

The meat that Jesus gave us is the WORD. The WORD is Jesus." In the beginning was the Word and the Word was with God and the Word was God. The same was in the beginning with God. All things were made by him; and without him was

88

not any thing made that was made. And the Word was made flesh and dwelt among us." All the power we need is in the Word.

Jesus asks this question of us..." Do you not therefore err because, ye know not the scriptures, nor the power there of?"

The power that we need is accepting by choice the New Covenant, and knowing the promises of that covenant sworn to us by God; and Guaranteed to us by the blood of Jesus. Every time you pray a scripture of the New Covenant understand that the covenant is guaranteed to us by the blood of Jesus. All the power we will ever need to overcome and prosper in all things has been given to us. It was a free gift all that is required is that we believe. Here are the keys to the new covenant:

John 1:17 "for the law came through Moses, but grace and truth came through Jesus"

John 1:12 "But as many as received him, to them gave he the power to become the sons of God, even to them that believed on His name."

John 6:29 "This is the work of God that you believe on Him whom He hath sent."

Ephesians 2:8 and 9..."For it is by grace (God's willingness ability and power to do those things for us that we can not or will not do for ourselves) that you have been saved. (In every way. From whatever you need to be saved) By faith (choosing to live one moment at a time with joyful expectation of the things that you cannot see) and that is not of yourself. It is a gift from God not of works lest any man should boast. "

Here are some New Covenant promises any of which would take care of all of your needs:

John 14:12-14 "Verily, verily I say unto you, that he who believeth on me, the works that I do shall he do also and greater than these shall he do; because I go to my Father. And whatsoever you shall ask in my name, that will I do that the Father may be glorified in the Son. If ye shall ask anything in My name, I will do it".

John 16:13 "Howbeit when He, the Spirit of truth is come, He will guide you into all truth; for he shall not speak of himself; but whatsoever He shall hear, that shall he speak; and he will show you things to come, He shall glorify me; for he shall receive of mine and shall show it unto you."

John 16:24 "Hitherto have ye asked nothing in my name; ask that you may receive that your joy may be full."

Mark 11:23and 24..."For verily I say unto you, That whosoever shall say unto this mountain, Be thous removed and be thou cast into the sea and does not believe that those things which he saith shall come to pass; he shall have whatsoever he saith, Therefore, I say unto you, whatsoever things you desire, when you pray, believe that you receive and you shall have them."

Finally, Here are some thoughts about how to walk in Power from Paul our teacher selected by God anointed by Jesus and taught of the Holy Spirit.

"That ye be not slothful (stand strong and don't give in to fear) but followers of them who through faith (Choosing to live one moment at a time with joyful expectation of the things that we cannot see) and patience (making a decision to believe the promises of God without demanding a sign or that we see them.) INHERIT THE PROMISES."

A teacher of the gospel recently stated that he did not understand why Christians were not seeing the promises of God coming to reality in their lives. Here is the answer precisely from Paul.

Galatians 4:10 "For as many of you as are of the works of the Law (made a decision to base your relationship with God on your performance in any way) are under the curse; for it is written, cursed is every one that continueth not in ALL things which are written in the book of the Law to do them. But that no man is justified by the law in the sight of God, it is evident for the just shall live by faith".

The ultimate dire warning comes again from our teacher Paul. Galatians 5:4 "JESUS IS BECOME OF NO EFFECT UNTO YOU, WHOSOEVER OF YOU ARE JUSTIFIED BY THE LAW ; YE ARE FALLEN FROM GRACE." There it is! Most of the body of Jesus have placed ourselves under the law and have fallen from grace, which is the new covenant. When we try to please God by our performance, we have refused to accept the completeness of the blood of Jesus and have rejected eating His Flesh.

Clearly, Jesus is telling us that all we need do to please God is to believe on Him and that is a moment by moment decision we make, by which we inherit the promises.

About the Author

Allen Fleming is the Pastor of Throne of Grace Ministries, Inc. Throne of Grace Ministries operates the websites: KnowJesusKnowGrace. Com and ThroneofGraceMinistries.com.

Allen is an author, teacher and minister of the truth of the Gospel of Jesus. He has been called into ministry by the Holy Spirit, for the purpose of communicating the unedited Word of God to the children of God.

His goal is to teach all people that their relationship with God is based on the complete work of Jesus and not on their performance.

He wants to see the children of God walking in the inheritance promised in the teachings of Jesus and guaranteed by His blood.

Write to Allen at <u>pastorallen@KnowJesusKnowGrace.com</u> or at

Pastor Allen Fleming

Know Jesus Know Grace.com

Throne of Grace ministries.com

Throne of Grace

P.O.BOX669153

Marietta, Georgia 30066

Throne of Grace Ministries is a 501c3 ministry offerings are deductible. If you have been led to make and offering and help us continue our teaching ministry. You may make your check payable to Throne of Grace and send it to the P.O.BOX above. Or you may make a secure on line offering at throneofgraceministries.com.

29826603R00063

Made in the USA
San Bernardino, CA
30 January 2016